ABOUT MAGIC READERS

ABDO continues its commitment to quality books with the nonfiction Magic Readers series. This series includes three levels of books to help students progress to being independent readers while learning factual information. Different levels are intended to reflect the stages of reading in the early grades, helping to select the best level for each individual student.

Level 1: Books with short sentences and familiar words or patterns to share with children who are beginning to understand how letters and sounds go together.

Level 2: Books with longer words and sentences and more complex language patterns with less repetition for progressing readers who are practicing common words and letter sounds.

Level 3: Books with more developed language and vocabulary for transitional readers who are using strategies to figure out unknown words and are ready to learn information more independently.

These nonfiction readers are aligned with the Common Core State Standards progression of literacy, following the sequence of skills and increasing the difficulty of language while engaging the curious minds of young children. These books also reflect the increasing importance of reading informational material in the early grades. They encourage children to read for fun and to learn!

Hannah E. Tolles, MA Reading Specialist

www.abdopublishing.com

Published by Magic Wagon, a division of ABDO, PO Box 398166, Minneapolis, Minnesota 55439. Copyright © 2015 by Abdo Consulting Group, Inc. International copyrights reserved in all countries. No part of this book may be reproduced in any form without written permission from the publisher. Magic Readers™ is a trademark and logo of Magic Wagon.

Printed in the United States of America, North Mankato, Minnesota.
062014
092014

Cover Photo: Thinkstock
Interior Photos: iStockphoto, Thinkstock

Written and edited by Rochelle Baltzer, Heidi M. D. Elston,
 Megan M. Gunderson, and Bridget O'Brien
Illustrated by Candice Keimig
Designed by Candice Keimig and Jillian O'Brien

Library of Congress Cataloging-in-Publication Data

Gunderson, Megan M., 1981- author.
 Bears eat and grow / written and edited by Megan M. Gunderson [and three others] ; designed and illustrated by Candice Keimig.
  pages cm. -- (Magic readers. Level 2)
 Audience: Ages 5-8.
 ISBN 978-1-62402-058-2
1. Grizzly bear--Juvenile literature. 2. Bear cubs--Juvenile literature. I. Keimig, Candice, illustrator. II. Title.
 QL737.C27G865 2015
 599.784--dc23
                    2014007943

Magic Readers

level
2

Bears
Eat and Grow

By Megan M. Gunderson
Illustrated photos by Candice Keimig

Magic Readers

An Imprint of Magic Wagon
www.abdopublishing.com

This is a baby bear.

It is called a cub.

Bears sometimes have twins.

The cubs tumble and roll
around together.

Cubs drink their mother's milk.

The cubs stay with their
mother as they grow.

A mother bear cares for her cubs.

She teaches them how to find food.

Bears eat plants and meat.

They eat berries, nuts, grasses, and honey.

Grizzly bears eat fish and bugs.

They also hunt elk, moose, and deer.

Elk

Moose

Deer

In summer and fall, grizzlies can eat 90 pounds of food a day.

In winter, they do not eat.

They sleep!

Grizzly bears are huge.

They can weigh up to 600
pounds.

A grizzly bear can be 8 feet long.

Standing up, it can be 10 feet tall.

A full-grown male grizzly is called a boar.

A female is called a sow.

Grizzly bears can live 25 years.